Mum was going to make a cake. She wanted Kipper to help.

First Mum gave Kipper an apron. Then she looked at his hands.
"What dirty hands!" said Mum

Mum looked at Kipper's nails. Kipper's nails were long.
"Let me cut them," said Mum.

Kipper made a fuss. He didn't want Mum to cut his nails. He didn't want to wash his hands.

"I must cut your nails," said Mum
"No! No! No!" said Kipper and he
ran out of the room.

Kipper ran into Biff's room. Biff looked at Kipper's long dirty nails. "Yuk!" said Biff. "You look like a troll."

"It's not fair," said Kipper. But then the key began to glow. It was time for a magic adventure.

The magic took them to a stream.
There was a bridge over the stream.

Biff wanted to cross the bridge.
"We can pick the flowers over there,"
she said. "Come on!"

Kipper ran after Biff. But there were trolls under the bridge.

Suddenly the trolls jumped out.
"Oh no!" said Kipper. "Trolls can be nasty."

"Hip, hip, hooray!" sang the trolls. "This is the troll bridge. Do come across."

“Will you eat us up?” said Kipper.
“No! No! We will not,” sang the trolls.

"We are not nasty," said a troll. "We just look nasty."

"Nobody likes us," said a troll. "We want to have a party but nobody wants to come."

The trolls went under the bridge. They got the party food and set out the party.

"Tuck in," said a troll.
The trolls had long dirty nails.

“Yuk!” said Kipper. “Look at her long, dirty nails.”

“Look at the troll food,” said Biff.

"Have a slug bun," said a troll, "or some slime jelly."

“Have a mud mint,” said another troll. “Mud mints are yummy.”
“Yuk!” said Biff.

"Have some bug pie," said a troll.
"Yuk!" said Kipper. "Look at his hands."

Suddenly the key began to glow. The adventure was over.
"At last," said Kipper.

The magic took them home. Kipper washed his hands. Then he went to get his nails cut.

“I’m not a troll,” said Kipper. “Trolls have dirty hands and long nails! Yuk!”